The Cost of Living: Surviving in a Broken System

Proudly Presented By:-

JWH Jr.

Legal Notice:- *This book is for informational purposes only. While every attempt has been made to verify the information provided in this book, neither the author nor the distributor assume any responsibility for errors or omissions. Any slights of people or organizations are unintentional and the Development of this book is bona fide. This book has been distributed with the understanding that we are not engaged in rendering technical, legal, accounting or other professional advice. In no event will the author and/or marketer be liable for any direct, indirect, incidental, consequential or other loss or damage arising out of the use of this document by any person, regardless of whether or not informed of the possibility of damages in advance.*

Copyright © 2024 JWH Jr.

Table of Contents

The Cost of Living: Surviving in a Broken System...............1

    Introduction:..10

    Chapter 1: Understanding the Broken System: An Overview..14

        1.1 Historical Context...15

        1.2 Current Economic Realities................................16

        1.3 Intersectionality and Vulnerability......................17

        1.4 The Importance of Solidarity..............................18

        1.5 Conclusion..18

    Chapter 2: The Financial Crisis: A Historical Perspective 19

        2.1 The Build-Up: Early 2000s Housing Boom............20

        2.2 The Collapse: Unraveling the Housing Market.....21

        2.3 Consequences on Families and Communities.......22

        2.4 Government Response and Regulatory Reforms...23

        2.5 The Long-Term Impact on the Cost of Living........24

        2.6 Conclusion..25

    Chapter 3: Income Inequality: The Growing Divide.......25

        3.1 Defining Income Inequality..................................26

        3.2 The Impact of Globalization and Technological Change..27

        3.3 The Role of Education in Income Inequality.........27

The Cost Of Living

3.4 The Effects of Political and Economic Policies......28
3.5 The Social and Health Implications of Inequality. 29
3.6 The Call for Systemic Change..............................30
3.7 Conclusion...30
Chapter 4: The Role of Education in Economic Survival 31
4.1 The Crucial Role of Education............................31
4.2 Disparities in Educational Access.......................32
4.3 The Burden of Student Debt...............................33
4.4 Education as a Tool for Social Mobility................34
4.5 The Role of Lifelong Learning.............................34
4.6 The Need for Systematic Reforms.......................35
4.7 Conclusion...36
Chapter 5: Healthcare Challenges: Access versus Affordability...37
5.1 The State of U.S. Healthcare..............................37
5.2 The High Cost of Healthcare...............................38
5.3 The Impact of Uninsurance and Underinsurance. 39
5.4 Health Disparities and Vulnerable Populations....40
5.5 Potential Solutions..40
5.6 The Role of Community Health Initiatives............41
5.7 Conclusion...42
Chapter 6: The Housing Crisis: Finding Shelter in a Tough Market...43
6.1 The Current State of Housing in America............43
6.2 The Impact of Rising Rents and Home Prices.......44
6.3 The Role of Institutional Investment....................45
6.4 The Lack of Affordable Housing Programs...........46
6.5 Potential Solutions to the Housing Crisis.............46

    6.6 Emphasizing a Right to Housing..........................47
    6.7 Conclusion..48
Chapter 7: Job Insecurity: The Gig Economy and Its Implications...49
    7.1 The Emergence of the Gig Economy....................49
    7.2 The Dark Side of Flexibility................................50
    7.3 The Burden of Unsustainable Conditions..............51
    7.4 The Role of Technology......................................51
    7.5 Navigating Government Regulations...................52
    7.6 The Importance of Organizing............................53
    7.7 Conclusion..54
Chapter 8: Food Insecurity: Nutrition in a Time of Scarcity...54
    8.1 The Current Landscape of Food Insecurity...........55
    8.2 The Consequences of Food Insecurity.................55
    8.3 Systemic Causes of Food Insecurity....................56
    8.4 The Role of Government and Social Programs.....57
    8.5 Community-Based Solutions..............................58
    8.6 Advocacy for Systemic Change..........................58
    8.7 Conclusion..59
Chapter 9: The Psychological Toll: Stress and Mental Health..60
    9.1 Understanding the Link between Financial Stress and Mental Health..60
    9.2 The Effects of Job Insecurity on Mental Health....61
    9.3 The Stigma surrounding Mental Health................62
    9.4 The Importance of Access to Mental Health Services..63

9.5 Employee Well-being and Workplace Mental Health 64

9.6 Community Support and Resilience 64

9.7 Conclusion 65

Chapter 10: Building Community: Support Networks and Resources 66

10.1 The Necessity of Community Support 66

10.2 Grassroots Initiatives and Mutual Aid 67

10.3 Community Resources and Assistance Programs 68

10.4 Engaging Local Organizations 68

10.5 Strengthening Neighborly Connections 69

10.6 Enhancing Civic Engagement 70

10.7 Conclusion 71

Chapter 11: Government Assistance Programs: A Help or a Hindrance? 71

11.1 The Purpose of Government Assistance Programs 72

11.2 Evaluating Efficacy and Reach 72

11.3 Barriers to Accessing Assistance 73

11.4 The Impact of Limited Funding 74

11.5 Alternatives and Innovations in Assistance 75

11.6 The Role of Community Organizations 75

11.7 Conclusion 76

Chapter 12: Personal Finance: Practical Strategies for Survival 77

12.1 Understanding the Importance of Financial Literacy...77
12.2 Budgeting Basics..78
12.3 The Importance of Emergency Savings..............79
12.4 Navigating Debt Responsibly..........................79
12.5 Exploring Income Opportunities......................80
12.6 Understanding Credit and Its Impact................81
12.7 Conclusion..81

Chapter 13: Activism and Advocacy: Fighting for Change 82
13.1 The Power of Collective Action........................82
13.2 Grassroots Movements for Change...................83
13.3 Engaging in Local Activism..............................84
13.4 Utilizing Digital Platforms for Advocacy............84
13.5 Partnering with Established Organizations........85
13.6 Navigating Challenges in Advocacy...................86
13.7 Conclusion..86

Chapter 14: The Future of Work: Adapting to a Changing Economy..87
14.1 The Evolution of Work......................................87
14.2 The Impact of Automation and Artificial Intelligence..88
14.3 Seeking Reskilling and Upskilling Opportunities 89
14.4 Embracing Flexibility in Work Arrangements.....89
14.5 The Importance of Well-being in the Workplace.90

14.6 Collaborative Approaches to Innovation............91
14.7 Conclusion..91
Chapter 15: Navigating the System: Stories of Resilience
....92
15.1 Voices of Resilience..92
15.2 Transformative Community Engagement...........93
15.3 The Role of Mentorship and Support.................94
15.4 Embracing Adaptability and Innovation..............94
15.5 Advocating for Change.....................................95
15.6 Building Hope Through Resilience.....................95
15.7 Conclusion...96

Introduction:

In the heart of every metropolis, the shimmer of prosperity dances just out of reach for millions. The undeniable truth is that the cost of living has skyrocketed, while many are left grappling with grim realities in a system that often feels fundamentally broken. For countless individuals and families across the United States, survival has become an intricate balancing act of finances, well-being, and personal aspirations. In this context, "The Cost of Living: Surviving in a Broken System" serves as an exploration of the challenges faced by so many, while also offering insights into the resilience and resourcefulness required to navigate these turbulent waters.

The phrase "cost of living" is often used as a catch-all to denote the various expenses one must incur to maintain their standard of life. Yet, stripping it down reveals a stark reality of soaring prices in housing, healthcare, food, transportation, and education—essential components integral to the fabric of everyday life. Meanwhile, wages have stagnated, and job security has all but vanished for many workers. The result? Families forced to make inconceivable choices, such as deciding between filling a prescription or putting food on the table.

The Cost Of Living

This book aims to illuminate the multifaceted issues surrounding the cost of living while drawing a vivid picture of the daily realities faced by those who struggle against a backdrop of systemic inefficiencies.

As we dissect the layers of this broken system, it becomes evident that socio-economic factors do not exist in a vacuum. Instead, they interweave to create compounded challenges, often trapping individuals and families in cyclical poverty. From soaring student loan debts that anchor young adults to a lifetime of financial struggle to the crisis of affordable housing that forces families into overcrowded and unsafe living conditions, our exploration reveals the deep fissures within the socio-economic landscape.

Moreover, we delve into the role of education in creating pathways for mobility—or the lack thereof—and how inadequate educational opportunities further entrench living costs. The disparity in educational quality, influenced by geographical and socio-economic factors, perpetuates a cycle where too many remain unequipped to navigate the myriad of economic challenges facing them. This disconnect is essential to understand.

The psychological implications of this struggle cannot be overstated. Daily worries about finances can lead to anxiety, depression, and a myriad of mental health issues that further complicate one's ability to manage life's demands. The toll on mental health pervades families and communities, often leading to a breakdown of social structures that could otherwise provide vital support.

Throughout this book, we will highlight personal stories of resilience—individuals who, against overwhelming odds, have carved out spaces of survival and pride. These narratives will depict the human spirit's capacity to adapt and maintain hope in the face of insurmountable challenges. From grassroots community efforts to support networks and mutual aid, readers will witness the power of collaboration and perseverance.

In tandem, we will also cover practical avenues for navigating the current system, from personal finance management strategies to understanding government assistance programs. Each chapter is designed not only to inform but also to empower, providing readers with tools to assert agency amidst chaos and complexity.

As we embark on this journey through the broken system of living costs, it is crucial to acknowledge that the issues we face are not insurmountable. Change is indeed possible, driven by the collective voices of those willing to challenge the status quo and advocate for a system that prioritizes accessibility, equity, and sustainability.

Ultimately, "The Cost of Living: Surviving in a Broken System" is more than a mere examination of socio-economic challenges; it is a clarion call to action. It urges readers to recognize the interconnectedness of our experiences and the necessity of solidarity in raising awareness, demanding change, and fostering a society that truly values the dignity of all individuals. Together, we can explore solutions, demand accountability, and work towards a future where the cost of living does not equate to survival, but rather to a life filled with possibilities.

Chapter 1: Understanding the Broken System: An Overview

The phrase "broken system" is often used to capture the sentiment of disillusionment that many Americans feel towards the structures that govern our lives. This ubiquitous label encompasses myriad facets of our socio-economic landscape—education, housing, healthcare, and employment—all of which have become increasingly tenuous, particularly for the most vulnerable populations. To understand the cost of living today, one must appreciate the complex interplay of forces that have led to this current state.

1.1 Historical Context

To contextualize the present, we must first look back at the historical choices that led us here. The economic landscape of the United States has transformed dramatically since the post-World War II boom, characterized by a robust middle class and a growing social safety net. The booming economy of the mid-20th century provided unprecedented opportunities for upward mobility, and government policies aimed at supporting families played a crucial role. However, starting in the late 1970s and into the 1980s, we began to witness a shift in economic policies that would profoundly reshape this landscape.

The rise of neoliberal philosophy ushered in an era of deregulation, tax cuts for the wealthy, and reduced government spending on social programs. The belief that free markets could regulate themselves without government intervention became the dominant ideology. These policies disproportionately benefited the wealthy while decimating labor rights and protections, leading to a significant erosion of job security for many working-class Americans. This is particularly evident in the decline of organized labor and the resultant weakening of workers' bargaining power.

1.2 Current Economic Realities

Today, as we survey the economic landscape, we are confronted with stark realities of income inequality, insufficient wages, and rising living costs. According to research from organizations such as the Economic Policy Institute, the wealth gap between the richest 1% and the bottom 90% has widened drastically. The top 1% now holds more wealth than the bottom 80% combined. This disparity creates an environment where while executive bonuses soar, many workers are left earning minimum wage or struggling to break free from a relentless cycle of debt.

Access to basic necessities like housing, healthcare, education, and food is increasingly tenuous. Rising rents have outpaced wage growth, forcing families to make gut-wrenching decisions about where to live and how to afford their basic needs. The burgeoning field of gig employment offers flexibility but often exacerbates precarity, depriving workers of benefits such as healthcare and retirement plans—fundamental pillars that ground a stable life.

1.3 Intersectionality and Vulnerability

It is crucial to understand that the impact of a broken system does not manifest uniformly across society; rather, it intersects with race, gender, immigration status, and other social determinants influencing one's experience. Historically marginalized groups are often disproportionately affected by the challenges presented by a broken system. For example, women, particularly women of color, face significant wage gaps and job insecurity compared to their male counterparts.

Similarly, systemic racism perpetuates barriers to education, employment, and housing, trapping countless individuals within cycles of poverty.

This intersectionality reinforces the notion that any attempt to understand the cost of living must be informed by an awareness of broader societal inequities. The narratives we share will reflect these complexities and illuminate the multi-dimensional struggles that reside within this broken system.

1.4 The Importance of Solidarity

To move towards solutions, we must adopt a framework of solidarity—recognizing that the struggles faced by one group are indicative of deeper systemic flaws affecting all of us. Individual stories of hardship are not isolated incidents; they are reflections of a larger societal issue that demands collective attention and action.

From grassroots movements advocating for fair wages to community organizations that provide food and shelter to those in need, a growing landscape of activism and advocacy demonstrates that change is possible. Strengthening ties and fostering communities of support can empower individuals to address their immediate challenges while also working towards broader societal reforms.

1.5 Conclusion

As we turn the pages of this book, we embark on a journey to dissect the anatomy of a broken system and confront the realities it presents. Through understanding the historical context and current economic realities, we can become more equipped to advocate for change, support one another, and build a future where the cost of living is not synonymous with the struggle for survival. The road ahead may be challenging, but it also offers opportunities for learning, growth, and mobilization toward a more equitable society.

Chapter 2: The Financial Crisis: A Historical Perspective

The financial crisis of 2008 marked a significant turning point in the socio-economic fabric of the United States, sending shockwaves through an already fragile economy and exposing vulnerabilities that had been simmering beneath the surface. At the heart of this crisis lay a complex interplay of financial systems, regulatory failures, and common human aspirations for homeownership and economic stability. Understanding this crisis is fundamental in grasping the current state of the cost of living, as it serves as both a catalyst for public awareness and a precursor to the hardships many face today.

2.1 The Build-Up: Early 2000s Housing Boom

In the early 2000s, America was caught up in a housing boom fueled by low interest rates, accessible credit, and aggressive lending practices. Banks and financial institutions sought to capitalize on the growing demand for home loans, often prioritizing profitability over responsible lending. The allure of homeownership was marketed as a gateway to financial security and the American Dream. For many, it was seen as an attainable goal, fostering a culture of aspiration that permeated society.

However, behind this façade of growth lay systemic issues. Predatory lending practices began to thrive as lenders targeted vulnerable populations, often approving loans without sufficient scrutiny of borrowers' financial situations. These "subprime" loans, characterized by high interest rates and unfavorable terms, became emblematic of the reckless behavior present in the financial sector.

2.2 The Collapse: Unraveling the Housing Market

As housing prices soared, the economic reality began to diverge from sustainable practices. When interest rates rose, many homeowners found themselves unable to meet their mortgage obligations. The widespread defaults triggered a cascading effect, exposing vulnerabilities within financial institutions that had heavily invested in mortgage-backed securities. The bubble burst, leading to a dramatic rise in foreclosures and a plummeting housing market.

By 2008, the consequences of this collapse rippled throughout the economy, culminating in one of the worst financial crises since the Great Depression. Major investment banks faltered, stock markets plummeted, and consumer confidence eroded. The government intervened with multi-billion-dollar bailouts aimed at stabilizing the financial system, yet the costs of this crisis were disproportionately borne by average Americans.

2.3 Consequences on Families and Communities

The fallout from the financial crisis reshaped American households and communities in profound ways. Millions lost their homes, and foreclosures became a grim reality for families that had once dreamed of stable homeownership. The ramifications extended beyond housing; rising unemployment rates and economic uncertainty led to a sharp decline in living standards for many. Families faced stark choices—between rent and food, healthcare, and education.

The post-crisis landscape exposed the fragility of consumer debt and the limitations of the public safety net. Many individuals struggled to secure stable employment as jobs disappeared in industries hit hardest by the recession. The gig economy burgeoned, yet the lack of security within these roles offered little relief to those caught in its cycle. As stability evaporated, so too did any semblance of economic confidence, with families now fearing not only the loss of homes but also their expenses.

2.4 Government Response and Regulatory Reforms

In response to the crisis, the federal government implemented a series of measures designed to stabilize the economy and prevent a future meltdown. The Dodd-Frank Wall Street Reform and Consumer Protection Act, signed into law in 2010, aimed to regulate the financial sector more stringently, promoting transparency and accountability. One of the key outcomes was the establishment of the Consumer Financial Protection Bureau (CFPB), created to safeguard consumers from deceptive lending practices.

However, the response to the crisis also sparked debates on the appropriateness of government intervention. As the banks were bailed out, public sentiment shifted against a system perceived to favor Wall Street over Main Street. The contrast between the struggles of everyday families and the rescue of financial institutions intensified calls for systemic change and accountability. This disillusionment catalyzed movements like Occupy

Wall Street, which highlighted issues of inequality and demanded a reevaluation of the power dynamics at play in our economic systems.

2.5 The Long-Term Impact on the Cost of Living

The financial crisis ushered in a new normal for many families, reshaping expectations of financial stability and creating long-term repercussions on the cost of living. As wages stagnated, many were left grappling with the consequences of debt accrued during the boom years. For younger generations, the burden of student loans coupled with the toll of the crisis meant that homeownership—a hallmark of financial success—was increasingly out of reach.

This generational shift in expectations coupled with rising living costs has led many to rethink their definitions of success and stability. The traditions of saving, investing, and purchasing homes have been replaced by calculated risks and adaptations to a precarious economic environment. The pursuit of the American Dream now feels more like a mirage, ever-elusive and shaped by unprecedented economic forces.

2.6 Conclusion

As we navigate the complexities of the financial crisis and its repercussions, it becomes apparent that understanding this event is essential to grasping the current landscapes of our economic realities. The scars left by the 2008 crisis influence how families approach financial decisions, respond to economic pressures, and contend with escalating costs of living. By grappling with these historical lessons, we can better equip ourselves to advocate for systemic changes addressing the root causes of economic instability and inequality.

Chapter 3: Income Inequality: The Growing Divide

Income inequality has emerged as one of the most pressing issues in contemporary society, shaping the lived experiences of millions and fundamentally altering the landscape of the economy. In a nation that prides itself on the ideals of opportunity and hard work, the stark reality of a growing economic divide signals profound dissonance between rhetoric and reality. As we delve into the dynamics of income inequality, we will explore its drivers, far-reaching effects, and potential solutions.

3.1 Defining Income Inequality

Income inequality refers to the unequal distribution of income within a population, where a small fraction earns significantly more than the majority. This disparity has widened dramatically over recent decades, with the top earners capturing an increasingly large share of total income. According to the U.S. Census Bureau, the Gini Index, a measure of income inequality, has risen steadily since the 1970s, indicating a trend toward greater economic polarization.

Understanding this divide requires a look at the various factors contributing to the gap. Educational attainment, occupational opportunities, and geographical disparities intersect to create an environment where the wealthy can accumulate wealth at a staggering rate while many struggle to achieve even basic financial stability.

3.2 The Impact of Globalization and Technological Change

Globalization and technological advancements have played significant roles in shaping income dynamics. The rise of international trade and outsourcing has shifted many traditional manufacturing jobs abroad, leaving behind job vacancies filled increasingly by low-wage service sector roles. Automation is another critical factor; as technology continues to evolve, many middle-skill jobs have been lost to machines, further widening the economic chasm.

These shifts have disproportionately affected vulnerable populations—particularly those without higher education or specialized skills. Hence, while the economy has expanded, too many segmented groups remain sidelined, confronted by limited opportunities to participate in this growth.

3.3 The Role of Education in Income Inequality

Education—often heralded as a key to upward mobility—has both reflected and exacerbated income inequality. Higher education is correlated with increased earnings, yet access to quality educational opportunities is not uniform. Systemic barriers, such as public school funding tied to local property taxes, disproportionately disadvantage marginalized communities, entrenching economic divides.

Inadequate access to education sets the stage for generational cycles of poverty, as lower-income families often find themselves unable to invest in their children's educational pursuits. Student loan debt has become a significant barrier to financial stability for many young adults, compelling them into jobs that do not match their qualifications, perpetuating the income gap.

3.4 The Effects of Political and Economic Policies

Political and economic policies have historically influenced the trajectory of income inequality. Tax cuts favoring the wealthy and corporations have reduced government revenue and exacerbated disparities. The effective tax rates for the top earners have significantly decreased since the 1980s, with wealth increasingly concentrated in the hands of a few. Conversely, social safety nets have faced cuts, leaving many without crucial support systems.

Moreover, labor laws that once protected workers' rights have weakened over the years, resulting in diminished bargaining power. The decline of unions further compounds the problem, as workers find it increasingly challenging to negotiate fair wages and benefits. Without a robust collective voice, many are left vulnerable to wage stagnation and precarious work conditions.

3.5 The Social and Health Implications of Inequality

The effects of income inequality extend beyond economic realms, infiltrating social structures and interpersonal relationships. Communities plagued by poverty often experience higher crime rates, diminished access to healthcare, and limited social mobility. Health outcomes reflect these disparities. Individuals from lower-income backgrounds face higher rates of chronic illnesses and limited access to preventive care, leading to a cycle of poor health exacerbated by economic hardship.

Additionally, the psychological toll of living in a highly stratified society cannot be overstated. Constant threats of financial instability foster despair and anxiety, undermining overall well-being and contributing to a range of mental health challenges.

3.6 The Call for Systemic Change

Addressing income inequality necessitates a multifaceted approach aimed at systemic change. Policymakers need to prioritize education funding reform, create opportunities for vocational training, and invest in local economies. Tax policies should be re-evaluated to ensure equitable contributions from high earners while strengthening social safety nets to provide support for marginalized communities.

Advocacy and grassroots movements also play critical roles in challenging the status quo. By amplifying the voices of those most affected by inequities, we can ignite discussions that demand accountability, transparency, and equitable distribution of resources.

3.7 Conclusion

As we explore the widening divide of income inequality, it becomes clear that this issue transcends individual economic experiences; it reflects systemic failures that require urgent attention. The promise of the American Dream is increasingly distant for many, undermined by barriers that keep them from accessing opportunities for advancement. By acknowledging the intersections of education, policy, globalization, and social dynamics, we can better advocate for a society that values equitable access to resources and opportunity.

Chapter 4: The Role of Education in Economic Survival

Education has long been heralded as a catalyst for economic mobility and personal development. However, in today's complex socio-economic climate, the relationship between education and economic survival is nuanced and multifaceted. As we explore this critical intersection, we will assess the current state of education in America, its accessibility, and the ways in which it impacts the cost of living.

4.1 The Crucial Role of Education

Education fundamentally shapes an individual's potential for economic success. Research consistently shows that individuals with higher educational attainment tend to earn more, have lower unemployment rates, and experience greater job stability. In a rapidly changing economy increasingly geared towards technology and specialized skills, educational background holds considerable weight in determining one's financial trajectory.

Despite this, the benefits of education are not uniformly accessible. Socio-economic factors, geographic location, and systemic inequities often dictate the quality and availability of educational opportunities, perpetuating cycles of disadvantage.

4.2 Disparities in Educational Access

Access to quality education in America remains highly stratified. Public school funding is typically tied to local property taxes, disproportionately benefiting affluent neighborhoods while leaving lower-income areas with underfunded schools. Such systemic inequities compound over generations, affecting opportunities for upward mobility and perpetuating cycles of poverty.

As a result, students from marginalized communities often face barriers that hinder their academic success. Inadequate resources, larger class sizes, and a lack of qualified educators contribute to lower educational outcomes, limiting students' chances of pursuing higher education and securing well-paying jobs. This systemic disparity further illustrates the interconnectedness of education and economic survival.

4.3 The Burden of Student Debt

The soaring costs of higher education in the U.S. introduce another dimension of complexity into the relationship between education and economic survival. Rising tuition rates and the increasing reliance on student loans have created a landscape where pursuing an education can lead to debilitating debt. Currently, student loan debt in the U.S. exceeds $1.7 trillion, impacting millions of borrowers and hindering their ability to achieve financial stability.

The burden of student debt extends beyond the immediate impact on individual finances. It limits young adults' choices, often forcing them to delay major life decisions such as buying a home, starting a family, or saving for retirement—further perpetuating economic uncertainties.

4.4 Education as a Tool for Social Mobility

While the challenges are considerable, education remains a vital tool for social mobility. Programs that provide scholarships, mentorship, and vocational training can empower individuals to rise above economic barriers. For instance, trade schools and community colleges offer accessible pathways to gain practical skills, enabling individuals to enter the workforce with competitive advantages while avoiding burdensome debt.

Furthermore, initiatives aimed at increasing educational access for marginalized populations, such as the expansion of early childhood education and after-school programs, play critical roles in leveling the playing field. By investing in education as a public good, communities can foster an environment where individuals are equipped to navigate economic challenges more effectively.

4.5 The Role of Lifelong Learning

In a rapidly evolving economy, the concept of lifelong learning has gained renewed significance. Continuous skill development and upskilling are essential in an age where industries transform at breakneck speed due to technological advancements. Workers must adapt to shifting job requirements, necessitating ongoing education and training opportunities.

Employers, too, have a stake in fostering a culture of lifelong learning. Creating pathways for professional development and investing in employee training ultimately benefit organizations by promoting a skilled and adaptable workforce.

4.6 The Need for Systematic Reforms

To bridge the gaps in educational access and address the rising costs of higher education, systematic reforms are imperative. Policymakers must prioritize education funding to ensure equitable distribution and support programs that offer diverse post-secondary options. This may include expanding access to vocational training and apprenticeship programs, which are critical in preparing individuals for high-demand fields.

The dialogue surrounding student debt relief and reform is also gaining traction. Addressing the burden of student loans requires comprehensive responses, such as income-driven repayment plans and targeted debt forgiveness programs aimed at low-income borrowers. By prioritizing accessibility and affordability in education, the cycle of debt and economic instability can begin to break.

4.7 Conclusion

Education serves as a powerful mechanism for economic survival, shaping individual futures and providing pathways to opportunity. However, the existing barriers to equal access and rising costs must be confronted collectively—acknowledging that education is not just an individual concern but a societal imperative. By reinforcing the notion that education is a fundamental right, we can work towards a system that fosters equitable access, empowering individuals to withstand the challenges of the current economic environment and achieve lasting stability.

Chapter 5: Healthcare Challenges: Access versus Affordability

Healthcare is a fundamental right, yet in the United States, it often reflects a troubling paradox—while advances in medical technology and care have progressed, access to affordable healthcare remains a critical challenge for many. The disparity between access and affordability has created a landscape where individuals and families are often left to navigate a complex system fraught with barriers. In this chapter, we will explore the challenges within the U.S. healthcare system, examine the implications for individuals and families, and consider potential solutions to create a more equitable landscape.

5.1 The State of U.S. Healthcare

The U.S. healthcare system is characterized by its complexity and fragmentation. Unlike many developed nations that operate under universal healthcare models, the U.S. predominantly relies on a multi-payer system, where services are provided by a blend of governmental programs and private insurance providers. This can create significant disparities in access to care based on factors such as income, employment status, and geographic location.

While the Affordable Care Act (ACA) aimed to expand access, millions still remain uninsured or underinsured. A report from the U.S. Census Bureau indicates that in 2020, approximately 31 million Americans lacked health insurance, constrained by costs and unjustifiable out-of-pocket expenses.

5.2 The High Cost of Healthcare

The spiraling costs of healthcare in the U.S. contribute significantly to the challenges individuals face in maintaining access to necessary services. According to the Kaiser Family Foundation, healthcare spending reached $4.3 trillion in 2021, equating to roughly $12,530 per person. The high cost of prescription medications, hospital stays, and preventative care has become a burden for many families, often forcing them to make difficult choices regarding their healthcare needs.

These escalating costs can loom over individuals as they attempt to balance essential living expenses. Families are frequently left with the heart-wrenching decision of whether to prioritize healthcare or meet other basic needs like housing and food.

5.3 The Impact of Uninsurance and Underinsurance

For those who are uninsured or underinsured, the consequences can be dire. Without adequate coverage, individuals often forego necessary medical treatment due to cost concerns, leading to detrimental health outcomes. Conditions that could be managed with preventative care frequently escalate into emergencies—resulting in higher long-term costs, increased hospital visits, and worse health outcomes.

Moreover, the psychological impacts of navigating healthcare without insurance can lead to heightened stress and anxiety, further exacerbating the challenges individuals face in their daily lives. The fear of receiving a substantial medical bill can deter many from seeking treatment altogether, perpetuating a cycle of poor health and economic instability.

5.4 Health Disparities and Vulnerable Populations

Healthcare challenges disproportionately impact marginalized populations, including low-income individuals, people of color, and rural communities. Systemic barriers—such as institutional racism, discrimination in medical settings, and economic constraints—compound the health disparities that exist within these populations.

For example, racial and ethnic minorities frequently experience inequities in access to quality care, diagnostic accuracy, and treatment efficacy. According to the National Healthcare Quality and Disparities Report, Black and Latino populations have higher rates of uninsurance compared to their White counterparts, leading to a gap in health outcomes that highlights the urgent need for reform.

5.5 Potential Solutions

Addressing the challenges within the healthcare system requires comprehensive approaches that prioritize equitable access and affordability. Potential solutions include expanding Medicaid coverage, implementing universal healthcare models, and increasing government subsidies for private insurance. By centering accessibility, we can ensure that individuals and families are able to receive timely and quality care.

Furthermore, there is a growing need for innovative healthcare delivery systems that look beyond traditional models. Telemedicine has garnered attention for its potential to expand access, particularly for those in remote areas who may struggle to reach healthcare facilities. By leveraging technology, patients can receive treatment, consultations, and ongoing care without the added burden of travel and associated costs.

5.6 The Role of Community Health Initiatives

Community health initiatives play a pivotal role in addressing disparities and creating supportive environments that promote overall wellness. These programs often focus on preventive care, health education, and accessibility to services, empowering individuals to take control of their health.

By fostering partnerships with local organizations, community health initiatives can tailor their programs to meet the needs of specific populations. This approach not only builds trust but also enhances the effectiveness of health interventions, leading to better outcomes for individuals and families.

5.7 Conclusion

The challenges of accessing affordable healthcare underscore a broken system that leaves too many behind. As we navigate the complexities of healthcare in the U.S., it is essential to advocate for changes that prioritize people over profits, and allow all individuals equitable access to the care they need. By recognizing and addressing the structural barriers that perpetuate inequality, we can begin to reimagine a healthcare system that promotes health and well-being for all—one where affordability and access go hand in hand, ensuring that no one is forced to choose between their health and their financial stability.

Chapter 6: The Housing Crisis: Finding Shelter in a Tough Market

Housing is not just a basic necessity; it is a cornerstone of individual and community stability. Yet, in recent years, the housing landscape in the United States has increasingly become a reflection of the substantial economic disparities and structural challenges that characterize the lives of millions. The housing crisis has manifested in many forms, from escalating rents and home prices to a lack of affordable housing options. As we delve into this chapter, we will unpack the intricacies of the housing crisis, explore its root causes, and contemplate potential solutions.

6.1 The Current State of Housing in America

The U.S. housing market is characterized by a severe shortage of affordable housing, which has reached crisis levels in many urban and suburban areas. According to the National Low Income Housing Coalition, there is a shortage of nearly 7 million affordable housing units for extremely low-income renters. These staggering figures paint a stark reality for families who are increasingly pushed into precarious living situations.

Rapid urbanization and population growth further exacerbate the crisis, as demand for housing continues to outstrip supply. As cities expand, housing developments often cater to wealthier demographics, leaving vulnerable populations to navigate an increasingly competitive market.

6.2 The Impact of Rising Rents and Home Prices

Soaring rents and home prices have placed immense financial strain on families and individuals. In many metropolitan areas, rent increases often outpace wage growth, rendering housing increasingly unaffordable. According to Zillow, rents surged by an average of 14% in 2021 alone, significantly squeezing household budgets and forcing many into a cycle of financial instability.

As private landlords capitalize on market demand, many families face evictions due to their inability to keep up with rising costs. This instability can result in transitory living situations, drastically affecting children's education and community ties. Homelessness, once viewed as an insurmountable crisis, has also surged in many cities, a haunting evidence of the bear trap that economic pressures have created.

6.3 The Role of Institutional Investment

The increasing role of institutional investors in the housing market has transformed the dynamics of homeownership and rental opportunities. Large corporations, seeking to profit from the housing crisis, have poured capital into purchasing single-family homes and converting them into rental properties. This rise of corporate landlords contributes to the financialization of housing, where profit motives eclipse the need for affordable living spaces.

Many tenants report feeling stuck in precarious rental arrangements, as corporate landlords prioritize returns over tenant stability. The traditional notion of homeownership is likewise undermined by rising prices, making it increasingly difficult for first-time buyers to enter the market and establishing a generational divide regarding access to home equity.

6.4 The Lack of Affordable Housing Programs

Despite the pressing crisis, affordable housing initiatives remain insufficient to meet demand. Funding for housing assistance programs has faced ongoing political challenges, leading to a lack of resources for addressing the root causes of housing instability. The Housing Choice Voucher program, which allows eligible low-income families to access affordable housing, remains underfunded and inaccessible for many who need assistance.

Community development and affordable housing construction projects often encounter bureaucratic red tape, zoning restrictions, and a lack of political will. Outdated policies that favor development rather than equitable access perpetuate the housing crisis, making meaningful change a challenge.

6.5 Potential Solutions to the Housing Crisis

Tackling the housing crisis requires concerted efforts from government entities, community organizations, and advocacy groups. Policymakers must prioritize affordable housing development and increase funding for housing assistance programs.

Expanding the Housing Choice Voucher program and introducing legislative protections for renters can help prevent displacement and stabilize communities.

Innovative solutions such as mixed-income housing developments can also provide pathways for fostering diverse communities and ensuring an equitable distribution of resources. By integrating affordable housing into new developments, cities can promote inclusivity while addressing the urgent need for shelter.

Additionally, community land trusts offer promising models for housing stability. These nonprofit organizations acquire land and develop housing in order to provide long-term affordability, thus removing housing from the speculative market. By involving the community in decision-making and planning, these models promote sustainable and equitable development.

6.6 Emphasizing a Right to Housing

At the core of any solution to the housing crisis is the recognition of housing as a fundamental human right. Advocacy for policies that prioritize housing equity and challenge discriminatory practices is essential in creating a system that prioritizes people over profits. Widespread public awareness campaigns aimed at destigmatizing affordable housing and condemning homelessness can help break down barriers to support.

By creating a cultural shift that values equitable access to housing, we can spark the necessary conversations to drive meaningful change and demand action.

6.7 Conclusion

The housing crisis in America unveils the complexities of a system deeply fractured by economic inequalities and structural challenges. As families grapple with soaring costs, it becomes increasingly crucial to advocate for equitable solutions that prioritize affordable housing access and stability. By dismantling the barriers to housing and fostering an environment that recognizes shelter as a basic right, we can build stronger, more resilient communities where individuals and families can thrive.

Chapter 7: Job Insecurity: The Gig Economy and Its Implications

The traditional landscape of employment has undergone an extraordinary transformation over the past few decades, giving rise to what is often termed the gig economy. As more workers find themselves engaged in temporary, flexible, and freelance roles, the implications of this shift on job security and income stability are profound. In this chapter, we will explore the gig economy's growth, its impact on workers, and the structural challenges that accompany this new landscape.

7.1 The Emergence of the Gig Economy

Characterized by short-term contracts, freelance work, and temporary positions, the gig economy represents a departure from conventional employment models. With the advent of technology and globalization, platforms such as Uber, Airbnb, and Fiverr have emerged, connecting workers with consumers in novel ways. In fact, a 2021 report from McKinsey estimated that nearly one in three U.S. workers have engaged in some form of independent work.

For many, the gig economy provides flexibility and the opportunity for supplementary income. However, its rapid growth has also led to a deeper concern regarding job security and benefits, which are often lacking in these arrangements.

7.2 The Dark Side of Flexibility

While the gig economy offers flexibility, it also breeds significant instability. Gig workers often lack essential benefits that traditional employees enjoy, such as healthcare, retirement plans, and paid time off. The absence of a safety net means that those dependent on gig work face vulnerabilities during economic downturns or personal crises.

Without guaranteed income, many gig workers struggle to budget effectively, with fluctuations in pay creating a precarious financial situation. As a result, a significant portion of the workforce risks falling into deeper financial insecurity while attempting to make ends meet. The stark reality is that the promise of flexible work does not necessarily provide the security needed for families and individuals to thrive.

7.3 The Burden of Unsustainable Conditions

Gig economy workers often find themselves navigating unsustainable working conditions, grappling with long hours and unpredictable hours. Drivers for rideshare companies, for example, may spend extended periods waiting for passengers to secure a few short rides, leading to exhaustion and stress. Coverage for expenses like fuel, maintenance, and insurance typically falls on workers, further eroding their earnings.

Moreover, the contractual nature of gig work often leaves workers in vulnerable positions, as the lack of job security can lead to exploitative practices. Companies may engage in tactics to minimize their accountability to workers—classifying them as independent contractors rather than employees, thereby evading responsibilities like wage guarantees and benefits.

7.4 The Role of Technology

The influence of technology has driven the rapid expansion of the gig economy, creating both opportunities and challenges for workers. Digital platforms serve as intermediaries, connecting supply and demand in real-time, yet they also perpetuate a system where workers compete for micro-tasks, optimizing efficiency over stability.

The pace of technological advancement raises additional questions about the future of work. The rise of automation threatens many traditional jobs and is likely to exacerbate existing inequalities, as those without the necessary skills to compete in the gig economy face decreasing opportunities. This dynamic highlights the paradox of progress: while technology has the potential to lift up workers, it also risks deepening existing disparities.

7.5 Navigating Government Regulations

The shift towards gig work raises critical questions regarding labor laws and worker protections. Current labor regulations often fail to accommodate this new reality, leaving gig workers without adequate safeguards. As companies assert that gig workers are contractors and not employees, questions arise regarding minimum wage laws, overtime protections, and the right to unionize.

Advocacy efforts aimed at creating fairer labor standards and reimagining workforce classifications are essential in protecting gig workers. Various states, including California with its landmark Assembly Bill 5 (AB5), have initiated efforts to reclassify gig workers as employees, but challenges persist across the nation regarding enforcement and implementation.

7.6 The Importance of Organizing

The gig economy's unique challenges underscore the urgency of organizing among workers. Collective efforts to establish worker rights and standards are critical for disrupting the cycle of insecurity. Successful campaigns, such as those initiated by gig workers in the rideshare and delivery sectors, have demonstrated the power of collective bargaining and advocacy when demanding fair wages and benefits.

Whether these gig workers have access to platforms for organizing or can collaborate across networks influences their ability to push for systemic reforms. Engaging local communities and forming alliances play crucial roles in fostering solidarity and building momentum for meaningful change.

7.7 Conclusion

The rise of the gig economy presents a complex and dual-edged sword, offering both opportunity and insecurity. As we navigate this new terrain, understanding the dynamics at play is pivotal for promoting fair labor practices and advocating for the rights of all workers. By recognizing the structural challenges that accompany gig work and emphasizing the importance of collective action, we can work towards a future where flexibility does not come at the cost of stability and security.

Chapter 8: Food Insecurity: Nutrition in a Time of Scarcity

The rising costs of living have far-reaching implications that extend beyond housing and healthcare, seeping into the daily lives of millions experiencing food insecurity. Defined as the lack of consistent access to enough food for an active and healthy life, food insecurity poses significant challenges in fulfilling basic nutritional needs, impacting the overall well-being of individuals and families. This chapter will examine the complexity of food insecurity, its drivers, and the strategies needed to combat this pervasive issue.

8.1 The Current Landscape of Food Insecurity

Despite living in one of the world's wealthiest nations, food insecurity remains a harsh reality for millions of Americans. According to the U.S. Department of Agriculture, approximately 10.5% of U.S. households experienced food insecurity in 2020, meaning they struggled to access adequate food. This statistic represents not just numbers, but real families facing daily challenges and impossible choices.

Food insecurity often disproportionately affects marginalized communities, including low-income households, people of color, and rural populations. Structural inequities, such as limited access to transportation and resources, can exacerbate these challenges, trapping families in cycles of poverty that are difficult to escape.

8.2 The Consequences of Food Insecurity

The implications of food insecurity are wide-ranging and multifaceted, affecting both physical and mental health. Individuals experiencing food insecurity are more likely to face chronic health issues, including obesity, diabetes, and cardiovascular diseases. Limited access to nutritious food options often leads to increased consumption of processed foods, which are typically more affordable yet lacking in essential nutrients.

Moreover, food insecurity exacts a psychological toll. Families may experience stress, anxiety, and depression as they struggle to provide adequate meals. The constant worry about accessing food can impede overall well-being and hinder personal and academic performance for children, compounding the negative effects over generations.

8.3 Systemic Causes of Food Insecurity

The drivers of food insecurity are deeply rooted in systemic inequalities. The rising costs of living, compounded by stagnant wages, create a landscape where many families find it increasingly difficult to afford nutritious food. According to a report from the Economic Policy Institute, the rising costs of groceries have far outpaced wage growth, creating a burden for low-income families who allocate larger portions of their budgets to food.

Additionally, the increasing consolidation of the food industry has resulted in a reduction of local food sources and an over-reliance on food deserts in low-income neighborhoods. These areas, characterized by their lack of accessible grocery stores that provide fresh produce, exacerbate the barriers to healthy eating and contribute to food insecurity.

8.4 The Role of Government and Social Programs

Government programs play a crucial role in combating food insecurity. The Supplemental Nutrition Assistance Program (SNAP)—formerly known as food stamps—serves as a vital safety net for millions of households. However, despite providing essential support, SNAP benefits are often inadequate in addressing the rising costs of living and groceries.

In recent years, advocacy efforts have aimed to increase awareness about the necessity of expanding these assistance programs while ensuring that they reach those in need. For instance, initiatives such as the expansion of emergency food programs during the COVID-19 pandemic underscored the vital importance of government action during times of crisis.

8.5 Community-Based Solutions

Combatting food insecurity requires community engagement and innovative solutions. Food banks, community gardens, and local food cooperatives have emerged as powerful players in addressing hunger and promoting access to healthy food. These grassroots efforts often partner with local organizations to develop sustainable food systems that prioritize equity and availability.

Community-based programs can empower individuals while fostering a sense of belonging. By involving members in food production and distribution, communities can break down barriers to access while building resilience and support networks.

8.6 Advocacy for Systemic Change

Addressing food insecurity necessitates systemic changes that confront the root causes of inequality. Advocates are pushing for policies that prioritize food justice, promote equitable access to healthy food, and challenge the systemic barriers that perpetuate hunger. This includes pushing for higher wages, affordable housing, and comprehensive access to healthcare, as these intersecting issues compound the challenges of food insecurity.

Food sovereignty—a framework that emphasizes the rights of communities to access local, healthy, and culturally appropriate foods—offers a guiding vision for advancing food justice. By reclaiming control over food systems, communities can work towards creating sustainable solutions that address food insecurity at its core.

8.7 Conclusion

Food insecurity remains a pervasive issue that underscores the broader challenges of navigating a broken economic system. By understanding the complexities behind food access and advocating for equitable solutions, we can work towards a future where nourishment is a right, not a privilege. Through collaborative efforts among government entities, community organizations, and individual advocates, we can create a society where all individuals have access to the healthy food needed for a life of dignity and well-being.

Chapter 9: The Psychological Toll: Stress and Mental Health

In a society increasingly characterized by financial strain, job insecurity, and overwhelming living costs, the impacts of economic hardship extend to mental health and overall well-being. The psychological toll of living within a broken system often manifests as chronic stress, anxiety, and depression, threatening individuals' capabilities to navigate their daily lives and maintain meaningful connections. This chapter will examine the intersection of mental health and economic challenges, exploring the profound effects on individuals and families.

9.1 Understanding the Link between Financial Stress and Mental Health

Financial stress has become an omnipresent factor in contemporary life, profoundly affecting individuals' mental and emotional well-being. Research consistently demonstrates a correlation between economic hardship and increased rates of mental health disorders. According to a study published in the Journal of Psychiatric Research, individuals experiencing financial strain are significantly more likely to report symptoms of depression and anxiety.

The pressure to make ends meet creates a vicious cycle, where financial instability exacerbates mental health challenges, and heightened stress impairs one's ability to manage daily responsibilities. This interconnectedness highlights the urgent need to address both economic and mental health challenges as part of a comprehensive approach to well-being.

9.2 The Effects of Job Insecurity on Mental Health

Job insecurity represents one of the most prominent sources of stress for individuals and families. As the gig economy expands and traditional job security diminishes, workers often grapple with uncertainty regarding their employment status and income. Research has shown that job insecurity correlates with higher levels of anxiety and poor mental health outcomes, as individuals fear losing their source of income and their ability to provide for their families.

Existing studies suggest that the long-term effects of job insecurity can be profound, leading to chronic stress and diminishing personal resilience. This phenomenon highlights the necessity of fostering safe, stable, and equitable work environments that prioritize mental health alongside financial security.

9.3 The Stigma surrounding Mental Health

Despite the increasing prevalence of mental health challenges in society, stigma remains a barrier that prevents individuals from seeking help. Many feel embarrassment or shame regarding their financial struggles, compounding their reluctance to seek mental health support. This stigma often perpetuates isolation and despair, making it more challenging for individuals to access resources necessary for recovery and stability.

Promoting awareness around the importance of mental health is critical in breaking down these barriers. By creating supportive environments that destigmatize mental health challenges, we can empower individuals to seek help and develop coping mechanisms.

9.4 The Importance of Access to Mental Health Services

Access to affordable mental health services is a vital component in addressing the psychological toll of economic instability. For many, the cost of therapy and counseling is prohibitive, especially in the absence of robust insurance coverage. According to the National Alliance on Mental Illness, nearly half of adults with a mental illness did not receive treatment in the previous year, often due to cost barriers.

Addressing the gaps in access to mental health services requires systemic change, including expanding Medicaid coverage, developing community-based mental health programs, and advocating for increased funding for mental health initiatives. By emphasizing mental health as a foundational aspect of overall well-being, we can work towards creating a more supportive infrastructure.

9.5 Employee Well-being and Workplace Mental Health

Workplaces play a critical role in shaping employees' mental health and emotional well-being. Organizations must prioritize mental health initiatives that promote awareness, provide resources, and create supportive environments for employees. Practicing policies that foster work-life balance, offering mental health days, and providing access to employee assistance programs can significantly impact workers' overall mental health.

Additionally, fostering open communication within workplaces can create a culture where employees feel empowered to discuss their needs and access resources without fear of judgment. By investing in employees' mental well-being, businesses not only contribute to individual wellness but also enhance overall productivity, morale, and organizational success.

9.6 Community Support and Resilience

Community support networks play an invaluable role in addressing the psychological toll of economic hardship. Engaging in supportive networks—whether through faith-based organizations, peer support groups, or community organizations—can provide individuals with a sense of belonging and collective resilience. Such networks offer emotional support and practical resources, creating environments where individuals can share their experiences and find solutions together.

Creating community initiatives that prioritize mental health and provide safe spaces for individuals to share challenges can enrich bonds and help combat the isolation stemming from economic hardship.

9.7 Conclusion

The intersection of mental health and economic challenges paints a complex portrait of the struggles many face in today's society. By recognizing the psychological toll of financial strain and advocating for accessible mental health services, we can work towards fostering greater resilience and well-being among individuals and families. It is imperative to advocate for systemic changes that prioritize mental health as an integral component of overall health, emphasizing the importance of supportive environments, community engagement, and accessible resources.

Chapter 10: Building Community: Support Networks and Resources

In the face of economic instability, community support emerges as a powerful tool for combating the struggles associated with a broken system. Building a sense of collective resilience is essential for promoting well-being and empowerment within communities. This chapter will explore ways in which fostering community support networks can address the interconnected challenges of the cost of living and provide individuals with valuable resources to navigate these difficulties.

10.1 The Necessity of Community Support

The power of community support cannot be understated in the context of economic hardship. Research has shown that strong social connections can significantly alleviate the stress and isolation caused by financial struggles. Individuals with robust social networks experience lower levels of anxiety and depression, showcasing the importance of bonds and support systems in promoting overall mental health and well-being.

Community support can take various forms—from informal networks among friends and family to organized initiatives that foster collective engagement. Regardless of the approach, the central theme remains the same: building strong connections enhances individuals' abilities to navigate challenges and find the resources they need.

10.2 Grassroots Initiatives and Mutual Aid

Grassroots initiatives play a crucial role in empowering communities and providing necessary support to those in need. Mutual aid networks, which emphasize reciprocity and communal support, have gained traction in recent years as effective avenues for addressing immediate needs while fostering a sense of collective responsibility.

These networks often connect individuals who can offer financial, emotional, or logistical help to those facing difficulties. By screening for needs and rallying resources, mutual aid initiatives create sources of support that address various challenges, from food insecurity to housing assistance. They exemplify community empowerment in action, demonstrating the potential for collective solutions to build resilience.

10.3 Community Resources and Assistance Programs

In addition to grassroots initiatives, local organizations and community resources play essential roles in providing support to those facing economic hardships. Food banks, housing assistance programs, and mental health services are among the vital resources available to individuals and families grappling with instability.

Significant barriers, however, remain in accessing these resources. Many individuals may not be aware of the services available in their communities, while bureaucratic hurdles can hinder swift access. Efforts to raise awareness about existing resources, simplify the application processes, and ensure culturally competent services are critical steps towards enhancing support systems for vulnerable populations.

10.4 Engaging Local Organizations

Local organizations serve as valuable resources for building community connections and providing essential services. By partnering with schools, faith-based organizations, and nonprofits, communities can create collaborative frameworks that enhance access to support. These organizations often have established relationships with community members, allowing them to engage effectively and respond to local needs.

Investing in community organizations and recognizing their importance as hubs of support can amplify their positive impact. Creating opportunities for collaboration between organizations can help to streamline resources and improve overall service delivery within communities.

10.5 Strengthening Neighborly Connections

In many cases, the simplest yet most impactful community support can come from fostering neighborly connections. Building relationships among individuals in neighborhoods can create support systems that extend beyond organized initiatives. By cultivating a sense of trust and connection with neighbors, individuals can better share resources, offer assistance, and create an environment of mutual support.

Simple acts, such as sharing meals, participating in neighborhood gatherings, or forming support groups, can lead to genuine connections that enhance community resilience. This neighborly spirit can strengthen bonds, creating layers of support for individuals facing economic instability.

10.6 Enhancing Civic Engagement

Civic engagement is critical to fostering community resilience and advocating for systemic changes. Mobilizing individuals to become involved in community decision-making processes empowers residents to take control of their circumstances and influence local policies. Participating in community meetings, advocacy campaigns, and local initiatives allows individuals to voice their needs and contribute to discussions about potential solutions.

By fostering a culture of engagement, communities can drive positive change, ensuring that the voices of those most affected by economic challenges are at the forefront. Advocating for equitable policies and resources creates opportunities for communities to respond collectively to systemic issues.

10.7 Conclusion

The journey through a broken system can feel daunting, but community support networks emerge as powerful tools in navigating the challenges that arise from economic instability. By fostering connections, seeking out resources, and building support systems, individuals and families can cultivate resilience and confront the difficulties of the cost of living head-on. The strength of community lies in its ability to uplift one another—together, we can work towards a future where everyone has access to the support and resources necessary to thrive.

Chapter 11: Government Assistance Programs: A Help or a Hindrance?

The role of government assistance programs is often a contentious topic, igniting debates regarding their effectiveness, accessibility, and implications for individuals in need. As economic challenges persist, understanding the complexities surrounding government assistance becomes critical in examining how these programs can be reformed to better serve those who rely on them. In this chapter, we will evaluate the efficacy of these programs, the barriers faced by recipients, and potential solutions to enhance their impact.

11.1 The Purpose of Government Assistance Programs

Government assistance programs are designed to provide support to individuals and families facing economic hardships. These programs cover various needs, including food security, housing assistance, unemployment benefits, and healthcare access. By serving as safety nets, they aim to alleviate immediate financial struggles while promoting stability and self-sufficiency.

However, despite their intentions, persistent challenges remain regarding the adequacy and accessibility of support provided through these programs.

11.2 Evaluating Efficacy and Reach

A critical aspect of assessing government assistance programs is their efficacy in addressing the needs of vulnerable populations. Programs such as the Supplemental Nutrition Assistance Program (SNAP), Temporary Assistance for Needy Families (TANF), and housing assistance offer crucial lifelines for millions. However, many individuals may find themselves falling through the cracks due to stringent eligibility requirements or bureaucratic inefficiencies.

Evaluating program performance requires examining the extent to which these initiatives reach those who need them most, particularly marginalized groups. Studies indicate that many eligible individuals fail to utilize these benefits, often due to lack of awareness, willingness to sign up, or confusion about application processes.

11.3 Barriers to Accessing Assistance

Several barriers hinder individuals from effectively accessing government assistance. Complex application procedures, prolonged wait times, and additional documentation requirements create obstacles that dissuade eligible individuals from pursuing benefits. Additionally, stigma surrounding public assistance may lead individuals to avoid seeking help altogether, perpetuating cycles of poverty.

Moreover, administrative hurdles can impede access to assistance programs over time, as recipients may experience changes in eligibility or face abrupt cuts due to policy shifts. These challenges often create an environment of uncertainty that destabilizes all aspects of life for individuals and families struggling to make ends meet.

11.4 The Impact of Limited Funding

Limited funding is a persistent issue that affects many government assistance programs. The reality is that budget constraints often lead to cuts in essential services or insufficient support to meet the growing demand. As costs of living rise, families increasingly require assistance, yet programs struggle to allocate adequate resources to respond effectively.

The consequences of underfunding can be dire, forcing families to sacrifice basic needs for a chance at survival. Advocates argue that prioritizing funding for these programs is essential in promoting equity and justice for all citizens.

11.5 Alternatives and Innovations in Assistance

In response to the limitations of traditional assistance programs, some communities and policymakers are exploring innovative approaches to address economic challenges. Basic income programs, for example, are being piloted in various locations, providing unconditional cash payments to individuals regardless of employment status. These initiatives aim to enhance financial security and foster economic independence.

Similar models, such as universal healthcare access and public service programs, highlight the necessity of reimagining assistance structures. By prioritizing human rights frameworks, these alternatives aim to provide holistic support while addressing systemic inequalities.

11.6 The Role of Community Organizations

Community organizations often play a crucial role in bridging gaps between individuals and government assistance. By providing navigation support, outreach programs can help individuals understand available resources and guide them through application processes.

These grassroots initiatives create valuable partnerships, ensuring that citizens have access to the support they need while fostering a sense of community empowerment. Collaborating with local nonprofits and organizations can also enhance the efficacy of government assistance programs by encouraging collective advocacy for increased resources and improved policies.

11.7 Conclusion

While government assistance programs play a vital role in providing support to individuals facing economic challenges, persistent barriers and limitations necessitate reform and innovation. Evaluating the efficacy of these programs and advocating for increased funding and accessibility can ensure that those in need receive the necessary assistance to promote stability and well-being. By prioritizing a holistic approach that embraces community organizations and alternative support systems, we can work towards creating a more equitable landscape for all.

Chapter 12: Personal Finance: Practical Strategies for Survival

In a world where economic challenges are mounting, developing practical personal finance strategies can serve as a critical lifeline for individuals and families seeking stability. The ability to manage finances effectively offers the potential to navigate uncertainty, reduce stress, and plan for the future. This chapter will outline actionable personal finance strategies that empower individuals to take control of their finances amidst a broken system.

12.1 Understanding the Importance of Financial Literacy

Financial literacy is foundational when it comes to managing personal finances. Building knowledge surrounding budgeting, saving, investing, and understanding credit empowers individuals to make informed financial decisions. Unfortunately, many individuals lack access to financial education, leaving them ill-equipped to navigate critical aspects of money management effectively.

Promoting financial literacy initiatives and targeting marginalized populations can help level the playing field, allowing individuals to develop skills that enhance their financial well-being.

12.2 Budgeting Basics

Creating and maintaining a budget is the cornerstone of effective financial management. By establishing a budget, individuals can track income and expenses, identifying areas to cut back and prioritize spending according to essential needs. While budgeting may initially appear daunting, the process can be streamlined through budgeting apps and tools that make tracking finances more manageable.

Establishing a realistic budget that accounts for fixed expenses (housing, utilities) and variable expenses (groceries, entertainment) helps clarify financial priorities. By regularly reviewing and adjusting the budget, individuals can remain proactive and responsive to changing circumstances.

12.3 The Importance of Emergency Savings

An emergency fund is a vital component of financial survival, providing a buffer for unexpected expenses such as medical emergencies or job loss. Ideally, individuals should aim to save three to six months' worth of living expenses in an easily accessible account. However, this may be unrealistic for those living paycheck to paycheck.

Starting small, even with modest contributions, can pave the way for financial security. By automating savings into a separate account, individuals can cultivate a habit of saving without the temptation to spend, gradually building a safety net over time.

12.4 Navigating Debt Responsibly

Debt is a pervasive issue that significantly impacts individuals' financial stability. Whether stemming from credit cards, student loans, or medical expenses, high levels of debt can overwhelm individuals and families. Developing strategies to navigate debt responsibly is crucial in mitigating its effects.

To gain control over debt, individuals should prioritize paying off high-interest loans first while making minimum payments on others. Utilizing snowball or avalanche methods can help strategize debt repayment effectively. Additionally, seeking assistance from non-profit credit counseling services can provide guidance and resources for individuals struggling with overwhelming debt.

12.5 Exploring Income Opportunities

Enhancing income potential is another avenue for improving financial stability. Individuals can explore opportunities to increase their earnings through side gigs, freelance work, or additional training to enhance job qualifications. This not only diversifies income sources but also cultivates skills that may lead to more resilient career pathways.

In addition, participating in skills training and enrichment programs can empower individuals to pursue higher-paying jobs and advance their careers—reflecting a proactive approach to not just survive but thrive in a challenging economic landscape.

12.6 Understanding Credit and Its Impact

Maintaining a good credit score is essential for accessing lending opportunities, securing housing, and obtaining favorable interest rates. Individuals should monitor their credit regularly, dispute any inaccuracies, and work towards paying bills on time. Understanding credit utilization ratios and borrowing responsibly are critical components of managing credit effectively.

Moreover, individuals should be wary of predatory lending practices that can further entrench debt cycles. Recognizing the implications of loans and credit agreements can empower individuals to make informed decisions without succumbing to potentially exploitative terms.

12.7 Conclusion

In a broken system characterized by economic challenges, personal finance can serve as a cornerstone for empowerment and stability. By promoting financial literacy, establishing practical budgeting strategies, and prioritizing savings, individuals can take vital steps towards financial resilience. The journey toward effective financial management may have its share of obstacles, but with proactive approaches, individuals can navigate even the most challenging circumstances and build a foundation for a more secure future.

Chapter 13: Activism and Advocacy: Fighting for Change

As the realities of a broken system become increasingly apparent, the role of activism and advocacy in driving systemic change cannot be underestimated. Individuals, communities, and organizations are rising to challenge the status quo, demanding accountability and equitable policies that prioritize people over profits. This chapter will explore the importance of activism, examine successful movements for change, and highlight the avenues through which individuals can engage in advocacy efforts.

13.1 The Power of Collective Action

Collective action represents a powerful tool for influencing change and advocating for social justice. When individuals come together to share their stories and experiences, they create a formidable force that can challenge systems of oppression and demand accountability from institutions. Activism serves as a response to societal inequities and underscores the interconnectedness of struggles faced by diverse populations.

History has shown that social movements have the potential to effect profound change. From civil rights to labor movements, collective action has reshaped policies and transformed society's understanding of justice, equity, and human rights.

13.2 Grassroots Movements for Change

Grassroots movements have emerged as critical driving forces behind advocacy efforts. These movements often take root in local communities, focusing on specific issues that reflect the unique challenges those communities face. Issues such as housing access, food insecurity, and healthcare disparities have mobilized individuals to defend their rights and improve their surroundings.

Organizations such as the Movement for Black Lives and Neighborhood Assistance Corporation of America (NACA) serve as examples of grassroots movements working to amplify marginalized voices and advocate for systemic reforms. Their successes illustrate the potential for localized action to create ripple effects across wider society.

13.3 Engaging in Local Activism

Activism at the local level allows individuals to engage directly with their communities and address issues relevant to them. From organizing community meetings to participating in advocacy campaigns, there are myriad ways to get involved—ranging from raising awareness about local issues to demanding policy changes.

Joining local advocacy groups or coalitions can provide individuals with a platform to connect with like-minded individuals and share resources. Community-focused movements often emphasize collaboration, ensuring that voices from all segments of the community are heard in the pursuit of equity.

13.4 Utilizing Digital Platforms for Advocacy

The rise of digital platforms has transformed the landscape of activism and advocacy. Social media and online campaigns have made it easier for individuals to organize, mobilize, and raise awareness about pressing issues. Content sharing, online petitions, and virtual events can amplify grassroots efforts and reach new audiences.

Engaging with digital platforms enables advocates to share personal stories, connect with others, and mobilize support for various initiatives. The power of hashtags and viral campaigns can bring attention to critical issues, generating momentum and urging collective action.

13.5 Partnering with Established Organizations

Collaborating with established organizations can bolster advocacy efforts, providing individuals with additional resources and expertise. Local nonprofits, advocacy organizations, and civil rights groups often have the infrastructure and knowledge needed to drive change effectively.

Partnering with these organizations can enhance the impact of grassroots movements and leverage existing networks to campaign for policy reforms. Many established organizations provide opportunities for volunteers to contribute their skills and engage in various campaigns.

13.6 Navigating Challenges in Advocacy

Activism is not without its challenges. Activists often face resistance from institutions and those holding power within systems that perpetuate inequalities. Navigating the complexities of advocacy requires resilience and strategic thinking to create meaningful change.

Building alliances and fostering collaborations can enhance the strength of advocacy efforts, allowing individuals to unite behind a common mission. Understanding the historical and social context of the issues at hand can also inform strategies that resonate with broader audiences.

13.7 Conclusion

As individuals confront the realities of a broken system, activism and advocacy emerge as powerful vehicles for driving change. By uniting voices and mobilizing communities, collective action can challenge entrenched structures and demand accountability from those in power. In an era where economic uncertainties persist, engaging in advocacy provides an opportunity for individuals to reclaim agency and work towards a brighter future based on equity, justice, and access for all.

Chapter 14: The Future of Work: Adapting to a Changing Economy

As the landscape of work continues to evolve in response to technological advancements and economic shifts, understanding the future of work is essential to navigating the complexities of the modern economy. Change is inevitable, and as we grapple with emerging trends and challenges, this chapter will explore the implications for individuals, communities, and policy makers as they strive to build a more equitable and sustainable employment landscape.

14.1 The Evolution of Work

The evolution of work has been characterized by shifts in employment structures, labor relations, and the skills required for success. The rise of automation, artificial intelligence, and digital technology is reshaping industries and redefining traditional job roles. This wave of change has raised important questions regarding the future conditions under which work will be performed and the implications for both workers and employers.

In the past, stable employment often meant lifelong careers with established companies. Today's workforce is increasingly diversified, marked by shorter job tenures, freelance engagements, and gig work. These trends highlight significant transformations in how individuals seek employment and navigate career pathways.

14.2 The Impact of Automation and Artificial Intelligence

Automation and artificial intelligence (AI) are among the most significant forces driving change in the labor market. While technology has the potential to increase productivity and efficiency, it also raises concerns regarding job displacement. Jobs that rely on routine tasks are most vulnerable, while higher-skilled positions often require ongoing education and training.

Although advancements in technology create new job opportunities—particularly in fields that require innovative thinking and creativity—they can also exacerbate inequalities by displacing workers without the appropriate skills to adapt. Therefore, understanding the implications of automation and AI is paramount in shaping policies that address workforce transitions.

14.3 Seeking Reskilling and Upskilling Opportunities

To thrive in a changing economy, individuals must prioritize ongoing learning and skills development. Reskilling and upskilling initiatives play a critical role in empowering workers to adapt to emerging job demands and secure sustainable employment.

Employers, too, can benefit from investing in workforce development, offering training programs and educational resources that equip employees with the necessary tools to succeed. Organizations that prioritize learning culture foster a workforce that is adaptable and resilient in the face of change.

14.4 Embracing Flexibility in Work Arrangements

The rise of flexible work arrangements—including remote work, hybrid models, and freelance opportunities—offers workers new levels of autonomy and choice. These arrangements provide individuals with the opportunity to balance work and family responsibilities while creating paths toward financial independence.

However, the lack of clarity regarding employee rights and protections in flexible work environments risks perpetuating inequities. Advocating for fair policies that ensure equitable access to benefits and protections, regardless of employment status, is crucial in shaping the future of work that honors individuals' rights.

14.5 The Importance of Well-being in the Workplace

The future of work must emphasize the importance of employee well-being and mental health. As workers face increasing pressures from economic uncertainty and changing job dynamics, organizations must prioritize creating supportive work environments that address issues related to burnout and overall well-being.

Promoting mental health initiatives, fostering open communication, and encouraging a healthy work-life balance contribute to workplace cultures that prioritize employee satisfaction and retention. Organizations that prioritize well-being not only enhance job satisfaction but also improve productivity and loyalty.

14.6 Collaborative Approaches to Innovation

In an era characterized by rapid change, collaboration between public and private sectors is essential in addressing challenges related to the future of work. Governments, educational institutions, and businesses must work together to develop frameworks that support workforce development and ensure equitable access to opportunities.

Collaborative efforts can enhance innovation, leading to policies and strategies that embrace inclusivity. By leveraging diverse experiences and expertise, stakeholders can create adaptive solutions that benefit the workforce, bridging gaps and fostering broadly shared prosperity.

14.7 Conclusion

The future of work presents both challenges and opportunities that demand our attention and action. By engaging in proactive dialogue regarding the implications of technological advances, embracing lifelong learning, and prioritizing employee well-being, we can navigate the complexities of this evolving landscape. As we look toward the future, the vision for work must reflect a commitment to equity, innovation, and collaboration, ensuring that everyone can thrive in an era of profound transformation.

Chapter 15: Navigating the System: Stories of Resilience

In the face of economic challenges and systemic barriers, the stories of resilience that emerge from communities across the United States serve as testaments to the indomitable human spirit. This final chapter will explore the narratives of individuals and families who have navigated the complexities of a broken system, showcasing their journey and the lessons learned along the way.

15.1 Voices of Resilience

The strength of community lies in its stories. Each narrative represents the unique experiences of individuals who have confronted adversity and triumphed against the odds. By sharing these stories, we shed light on the diverse paths taken toward survival and empowerment.

Residents from various backgrounds have faced challenges such as unemployment, food insecurity, housing instability, and mental health struggles. Their resilience not only highlights the hurdles faced but also underscores the creative solutions and support systems that have emerged in unprecedented circumstances.

15.2 Transformative Community Engagement

Many stories of resilience begin with community engagement—individuals recognizing the need for support and taking the initiative to collaborate with others. These collective efforts have manifested in various forms, from organizing local mutual aid networks to participating in advocacy movements.

Through grassroots initiatives, individuals have connected with neighbors facing similar challenges, resulting in innovative responses that address community needs. By pooling resources and harnessing collective knowledge, these networks promote resilience and demonstrate the transformative power of solidarity.

15.3 The Role of Mentorship and Support

Personal narratives often feature mentors and advocates who play pivotal roles in guiding individuals towards opportunities and hope. Mentorship fosters connections that empower individuals to navigate complex systems, providing critical support as they pursue education, employment, and personal growth.

The impact of mentorship cannot be overstated; it provides the tools needed for success while fostering self-confidence and determination. Stories of individuals who have benefited from mentorship highlight the importance of shared wisdom in building resilience within communities.

15.4 Embracing Adaptability and Innovation

Resilience often emerges through adaptability. Many individuals have found creative solutions to navigate the challenges posed by a broken system. Entrepreneurs and artisans have developed businesses rooted in their skills and passions, illustrating the power of innovation in mitigating economic pressures.

These narratives of adaptation serve as inspiration, showcasing the potential for individuals to create their paths and reshape their futures despite overwhelming odds. The stories reflect a commitment to self-determination, emphasizing that resilience is forged in the face of hardship.

15.5 Advocating for Change

Many individuals' journeys also extend into the realm of advocacy, where personal experiences fuel the desire for systemic change. Those who have faced economic hardships often become passionate advocates for justice, using their voices to speak out against the systems that perpetuate inequities.

These advocacy efforts reflect a broader movement—a collective determination to dismantle the barriers that impede access to essential resources. Their stories fuel a narrative of resistance, serving as catalysts for change and inspiring others to join the fight.

15.6 Building Hope Through Resilience

At the heart of the stories we explore lies an enduring sense of hope. While the challenges of navigating a broken system can feel overwhelming, the reminders of resilience shine through. Each story reflects the human spirit's capacity to confront adversity and emerge stronger, reminding us of the collective power of communities in times of crisis.

These stories serve not only as personal triumphs but as calls to action. They remind us that, collectively, we have the power to reshape our systems and prioritize accessibility, equity, and justice for all individuals.

15.7 Conclusion

As we conclude this exploration of resilience within a broken system, it becomes evident that while challenges abound, hope endures. By listening to the stories of individuals who have navigated these struggles, we can appreciate the richness of their experiences and the potential for transformative change. Together, we can learn from these narratives, carry forward their lessons, and work towards a future where survival is no longer a struggle, but a shared journey toward collective flourishing.

The End